A Life of Whispers

Sara N. Abuljadayel

Published by Sail Publishing L.L.C.

First published in 2023.

This book uses a font and an alignment purposed to make the reading experience easier for dyslexics, towards an inclusive reading experience.

ISBN: 979-8-9893775-2-7

UAE National Media Council Permit #: MC-02-01-3721918

Age Classification: +16
The age classification for this book's contents is set in accordance with the age classification system issued by the UAE's National Media Council.

Email: info@SailPublishing.com
Facebook: facebook.com/SailPublishing
Instagram: @SailPublishing
Twitter: @SailPublishing

Table of Contents

I Wonder How It Ends

Although we wish for happy endings,
No matter what happens,
We still try to be realistic and accept the facts as we go along.
What's really hard sometimes, is how we anticipate the way the story ends.
Especially when we are in so deep, and it's hard to breathe.
I really wonder how the story ends.
How we will flip the pages and see the end.
I am used to telling the story after I see the ending.
Like a picture that was full and completed.
And only or mostly,
When I see the upside or the ending.
So this is a challenge;
As I start writing this book
I am writing the beginning, not knowing where to go next.

New-Age Life Lesson

Life is full of garbage,
So choose your garbage wisely.
Make sure that you can live with it as is.
Because there will come a time when you want to complain, and people will say:
You chose that!
Now shut up and live with it!
I am not talking about marriage or work or study, or friends.
I am talking about any choice and every choice you have to make.
Make sure you think it through as much as you can.
Because you will really have to live with it.
So, choose your baggage carefully.

Are We blessed or Cursed with Knowledge

Blessed are those who have knowledge and can use it in the time of need;
Yet cursed are those who knew too much and froze up and couldn't use it.
Sometimes although knowledge is power,
Foreseeing where every path will take you can cripple your movement and your decision to move forward.
Knowledge is useful.
Seek it.
Use it.
Apply it.
Learn from it.
But make sure you know where every piece belongs.
Too much knowledge, without knowing its right place, can be useless.
Look around.
Think.
Observe.
Apply.
And remember,
That memory will show you what to do next.
Are we blessed with knowledge?
Or,
Are we cursed for knowing too much?
How you use it will show you which is which.

When You Become History

Weird title, right?
A song actually sparked this!
Growing up in the generation where the 80s are now far enough back to be considered young;
I couldn't help but to think of where we were and where we are now.
I will never forget the day my daughter looked at the intercom phone and asked me:
Mama, what is that?
Moving along…
Listening to:
Band: Backstreet Boys
Song: Everybody (Backstreet's Back)
Released in 1997
I realized:
I have to write these details,
Because the current generation
Is 20 years younger than me,
And I am approaching 40,
And might not know who they are.
I just realized,
This was a time when we were the kids,
Now we are the parents,
Soon enough we will be the grandparents.
One day,
We were the future.
Now,
We are the present.
Then,

We will be the history or the past.
I don't know what to tell my kids.
All I can say is:
Be ready,
The cycle reaches everyone.
Think wisely.
Prepare thoughtfully.
Grow up cautiously.

I Am So Sorry

My dear me,
My dear you,
My dear friend,
My dear reader,
I am so sorry.
I am so sorry, deeply, and terribly, sorry.
It feels like I deceived you.
When times are bleak and life is hard,
I managed to draw a string of hope,
And a line of choice that you can hold onto;
And follow to brighter days.
I made it feel easy.
I was giving you shortcuts.
I found the ending and told you what to do to survive.
Little did I know;
When I decided to write the beginning
and the middle before reaching the end;
that it would be this hard.
I promise you the world.
I always have and always will.
But in the middle of the drama,
I just can't see it.
Not yet.
I didn't lie.
I never did,
So I won't lie now.
I guess I was trying to save you from the agony.
I guess I was trying to show you that it will all be OK at the end;
Even though it seems to be out of reach.

This book is different.
The story is new to you and to me too.
I am trying to find the shining sun in the middle of the misty clouds.
But I can't seem to see it.
But it's OK.
Because I believe it.
Because I have to believe it.
What else would I believe?
That this darkness will continue?
No, I can't.
I won't.
It won't stay.
Because life is a cycle of ups and downs;
Of dramas and dances.
I am waiting for the day I dance with Joy.
I know it's there.
I am still waiting for that door to open.
Meanwhile,
I am here.
Now.
Writing.
Living.
Moving forward.
in miniature steps.
And when the time is right,
I will leap.
And so shall you.

My Dear Kids

I need to mention my kids.
I am a mom.
I am a parent.
I can't help it.
They are an extension of me.
What I do affects them too.
My dear kids, oh my kids.
We are approaching shifting tides.
The world as we know it is changing,
On a large scary scale:
Threats of World War 3 are becoming serious (I hope it remains as talk only)
Global warming (I hope we find a solution soon)
Economic shifts (basically everyone's budget is running low but no one will admit it; I hope it gets better not worse)
New culture and tradition are becoming normal (well, conservative now seems old fashioned)
All of these scare me, especially the last point.

How will I raise you?
How can I tell you something is wrong when the whole world says it's OK!
it's scary!
I pray to God every day that I will know what to say and what to do.
I pray to God to help us do the right thing.
I pray all can be solved,
All can be healed,
And all can be achieved with the help of God.
I am scared, but I still have faith.

Life and Love

I keep thinking of my kids,
When I am faced with life's realities.
I keep thinking:
How can I help them to protect themselves from the heartbreaks that life will throw at them?
In a matter of days, I've seen some heartbreaks that kept me awake at night.
It's not easy.
The amount of energy invested in a relationship, then it all goes to waste.
Regardless of the reason,
Regardless of the stage of the relationship,
It still hurts.
Someone still ends up with a broken heart.
I hope you heal.
I hope you stand.
I hope you move forward.

All I can tell my kids is:
One day it will be a story to tell,
If you remember the details.
And you will find a way to heal and move forward from there.

Face the Tide

I wear my emotions on my sleeves.
Wait,
That doesn't sound right.
Because emotions come and go like tidal waves.
Some are soft and smooth,
Passing like a breeze.
Some are strong, fierce, suffocating like a tsunami.
Instead;
I wear my heart on my sleeve.
So every emotional burst,
I face with my heart first,
Then comes the rest of me.
That's why every changing wave feels like a reoccurring
tsunami.
It's draining.
It's painful.
It's exhausting.
I would tell you to take care of my heart when you see it,
But that's not the case.
No one carries their heart on their sleeves.
They know better.
I learned to know better.
I learned to hide it,
Behind my back.
I learned to lock it,
Inside of me.
I forbid it to see the world.
I forbid the world to see it.
I protected it well.

With time, I learned to slowly set it free,
To slowly get it to touch the gentle waves,
Wiped its tears when necessary, and hid it back again inside of me.

I taught it to glance from behind my back.
I taught it to stand under my protective arm, not further, not in front of me.
It's dangerous when that happens.
It's like a reckless child,
That still doesn't know that fire burns,
That still doesn't know that waves suffocate.
Every now and then,
It wanders off;
And I have to pick up its pieces and save it from the emotions tsunami,
And tidal waves of disappointment and despair.
It's better than it used to be.
It's recovering better now with practice.
But I still wear it on my sleeves.
Sometimes, I can't help it.
Sometimes, I just forget that I am.
If you ever see it, treat it with care.
Sometimes it's just a kid,
Looking for a connection,
Looking to explore,
Looking for more love and care than it has and can offer.

Where Are We Right Now

I am looking for joy that I can feel.
Happiness that I can touch.
Peace that I can see.
Serenity that I can believe.
With all that's going on,
It's hard to notice them so clearly.
So much is happening that it makes the lines unclear and blurry.
You can't tell what's right anymore.
Everything feels wrong.
Everything feels scary.
Hope is there somewhere,
But it's too foggy.
Too noisy.
Too crowded.
I don't know what advice to follow:
Stand still?
Push through?
Listen carefully?
Block out the noise?
Listen to your heart?
Listen to experience?
Do nothing?
Just breathe?
Great advice!
But do you do it all at once?
Or do none?
New times,
New measures.

My advice:
Keep it simple.
Boil it down to basics.
Look for necessities.
Then you will know how to move forward.

A Message From Me to You

I see that you are lost.
And that it's hard to say that you don't know.
Just keep trying.
You will get there.
Remember;
It's your fear that's holding you back.
Let go.
Keep trying.
Take it easy.
If you fail,
It's not the end of the world.
You can try again and again,
Until it gets better and better.
After all,
That is what you are preaching, isn't it?
So practice what you preach.
It won't be perfect,
But it will be more beautiful
than what your fear says it would be.

I Am Almost 40! Wait! What!

Yeah!
That's the conversation I had with a friend.
Of course, I said it to her casually,
But secretly, freaked out inside.
I suddenly heard myself say:
Wait! I am not yet there! There's still so much I want to do!
So I decided to make a mental life list of what I still wanted to do,
And I was surprised!
I realized that I mostly achieved all what I wanted in life.
Alhamdulillah, it gave me
Peace,
Joy,
Gratitude,
Pride,
A strange form of self-love,
And self-fulfillment.
But then I was confused…
So what's next?
Is that why I feel lost?
Is that why I feel dull sometimes?
Pointless, other times?
I mean, I had gone through my bucket list, mostly…
So what's next?
There should be more that I still want…
Well,
Mostly, I am out of energy these days,
So I won't push so hard.
But I guess I will make some new goals, that don't take so much effort as the previous things I did.

Let's see where they take me,
Or take us,
As I have to make sure they fit with my family.
I am OK being 40.
Looking forward to the new aging process that comes with it.
I plan to use it wisely.
I have to.
I want to and I will.
I have managed the previous 40; why should the coming years be any different.
From weakness to strength.
From down the hill to upwards.
I always find a way to keep moving.

Hey You!

Hey you, little one.
I see you there,
In the shadows.
Hoping not to be noticed.
Why the sad face?
Yeah! I see it! Great poker faces by the way!
But I still see your sad eyes.
Me: Why so sad?
Kid: It's a cruel world.
Me: I know. But hasn't it always been like that?
kid: I thought it was a bit more forgiving.
Me: Maybe it is, but you just have to forgive yourself first.
kid: People aren't so forgiving.
Me: Maybe they can't forgive themselves, so they project it onto others.
Kid: But that's so sad.
Me: Yes, it is.
kid: What can we do?
Me: Begin with yourself first.
The world will follow.
And remember the Qur'anic phrase:
"إن الله لا يغير ما بقوم حتى يغيروا ما بأنفسهم"

Stand Up

You've been broken for so long,
Collecting the pieces of your heart and soul.
Wondering how to fit in,
How to survive.
Get up.
Stand up,
And fight.
Stop taking the punches and punch back.
So what if you're tiny,
Weak,
Broken,
Damaged?
We all are.
So stop whining,
And fight back.
We get to places when we fight,
Not when we surrender.
You've surrendered for so long.
Yeah, it hurts,
Badly,
But get up anyway.
Stand up,
And punch your way through.
Beats the alternative,
Because you are in the alternative.
Now stand up and punch.
When you do that,
And punch your fear, pain, sorrow, agony;
You will realize that fear was only holding you down.

With a punch of courage,
And standing up,
Suddenly the fog clears;
And it's smooth sailing from there.
God knows it's scary and hard,
But we don't move forward while being afraid.
We move forward and we pull our fear behind us,
And we use our courage in our hearts,
The strengths in our fists,
And the insight in our minds to stand up and move through and move on.

I Am Sorry

My dear child,
I am sorry I don't smile too much.
Life happened to me.
I would love to smile and laugh and do fun things,
But life happened to me.
It took me places that I survived with a great deal of effort.
I am sorry I am gloomy,
But I am a realist.
Life happens.
God knows how much effort I put into changing and being where I am today.
To be honest,
Life happening taught me a lot of good lessons.
I am grateful for them.
I am stronger because of them.
I am humble, truthful, fair, reliable, and trustworthy,
Because I have seen the opposite of these traits and isn't pretty.
At least not by my standards.

I am sorry I don't smile much.
But I promise you,
That I am grateful to be where I am.
I am blessed to be who I am, and I will do my best to keep the past in the past.
But I really can't promise that I will laugh.
Maybe you should keep trying.
Who knows,
Maybe you'll succeed.

Come Back

Hey you, I see you there.
Hiding in the darkness.
Thinking it's your friend.
I don't blame you.
It feels safe.
Safer than being under the spotlight,
Feeling exposed.
I know you.
You can show people that you are smiling and happy.
You definitely can put on a show.
But when the crowd leaves,
And the lights are off,
You slowly retreat to that same spot in the shadows,
Where no one sees you,
Where no one seems to care to look.
It was what you were used to a long time ago.
You learned to live with it and deal with it.
It became your safe haven.
You got so used to it,
That getting out of the shadows scares you,
Not that light the scares you.
What if you get hurt?
What if the happiness is fake?
What if it doesn't last?
You convinced yourself to stay in the shadows.
No one can deny the disappointment and the pain you have gone through.
I see them keeping you there.
Hidden in the folds of shades around you.
But you are wrong.

You know you are.
Because you tried the light.
You tried the happiness.
It felt so warm.
So lovable.
Don't waste it.
Don't lose it.
Look for it.
Fight for it.
The shadows will be there anyway.
Just remind yourself it is worth more to you to be happy than to be sad.
You have the courage.
You can do it.
Just go ahead and smile.
It will be worth your effort.

40!

It's been a while since I last sat down and looked back at my life to see where I was,
Where I am,
Where I will be.
I was so hung up on everyday details,
That I didn't notice the world moving around me.
Until one day,
With a random conversation,
The number 40 is mentioned,
And I froze.
Well,
I am not 40 yet.
But it's one year from now.
That number used to haunt me.
I couldn't,
I can't,
Stop thinking about it.
I wonder what and where I expected to be at this age.
Is this what I had in mind?
Is this the 5 or 10-year plan people always ask you to make?
Is this where you see yourself when you are 40?
I am not confused or disappointed.
Not at all.
I am grateful to have achieved many of my dreams,
Even the ones people told me were impossible.
I am lucky enough that most of my bucket list is done.
But now what?
Should I suddenly have a new plan with a new goal?
I don't know.
I am still thinking.

Stand Up

Sometimes you fall down so often,
That you already know how to get back up.
Other times,
You fall down badly,
And don't get up easily,
But you have time to rise slowly.
All of this is doable,
Manageable,
Acceptable.
But sometimes,
You have a bad fall,
You don't have time to heal,
And you fall down again,
And again,
And again.
That's where you are in trouble,
That's why you are drained out,
Why the smallest problem
Feels like a disaster.
You didn't heal properly.
You didn't stand up right.
You didn't process and go through all what happened.
That's OK.
The most important thing,
Is that you notice it,
So you can shield yourself when you are down,
And cover your head on the way up.
You need to know where you stand,
Where you can fight,
And how to fight.

This way you will heal better,
Because too many falls is something new to you.
That's OK.
Notice it,
And stand up,
And stand tall,
And move on.

Set Yourself Free

Set yourself free,
My dear friend.
I know you are scared.
I sense your fear.
I feel your fear.
You are well guarded,
To stay protected.
But your saviors are your captors.
To protect you they have imprisoned you.
You've been through a lot.
God knows I know what you've been through.
My dear friend,
I know your pain.
I see your pain.
I feel your pain.
I know why you feel scared,
And I know why you want to feel protected.
I know why you don't mind being imprisoned.
It's the safest you have ever felt for a long time.
You forgot how to feel safe.
You forgot how to smile.
You forgot how to judge the character of those around you.
And when you finally found someone to trust,
Someone worthy of letting your guard down,
You actually let go of your fences,
You let them in.
They accept their duty,
For the love of you and the care of you.
They dedicated their life to protect you.
To make you happy.

To keep you safe.
They know your pain.
They want to walk you through it.
They want you to feel happy again.
But in doing so,
They imprisoned you.
Not intentionally,
But out of fear they unknowingly learned from you.
Please, my dear friend,
Look past your fears.
See those who would love to help you too.
See those who have good intentions and want to give joy and love.
There are people who want to see you happy.
See you safe.
See you free.
You know what?
By all means,
Go ahead and test them.
As much as you want, for as long as you need.
Until you are sure.
Then take a leap of faith,
And move forward from there.
Keep testing if you like.
It's your right.
But give way for a chance to expand your joy and safety circle.
There's so much love out there
That can take care of your fear.
I know the world is scary.
I had my share of drama and disappointment.

But I still saw faith, joy, dignity, humor, beauty, and so many things that make up for that drama.
For which I am grateful.
For which I am lucky to have seen through them.
Please give it a chance.
Please give yourself a chance.
You deserve more.
You are stopping yourself.
I know why.
But please try.
And set yourself free.

What Is Wrong with People

I mean really!

What's wrong with people!?

What happened to:
Dignity?
Respect?
Kindness?
Bravery?
Forgiveness?
Support?
Understanding?
Compromising?
Sharing?
Sacrificing?
Warmth?
Values?
Fairness?
Benefit of the doubt?

These were words used in the past,
As symbols for a trait valued in a person.
Traits that are preferred to be in a person,
But now it just seems like an imaginary value;
A story that you hear about.
It's not only sad,
It's frustrating really.
What's wrong with people?
Did they forget what it means to be kind?
What it means to give a chance?
What it means to try and understand?
What it means to have the benefit of the doubt?

Well, I have to be fair;
People changed.
To survive these days,
You need to test people.
You need to believe they are guilty until proven innocent.
You need to believe they are lying, and question them until you are sure they are telling the truth.
People changed.
It's hard to find someone transparent, so you can be transparent.
Is this what we want to teach our kids?
Is this how we want to live?
It's draining.
Unfortunately, that's how we survive.
We barely are.
Is this what it's come to?
I still believe in kindness.
In the values,
In all the traits that seem be lost.
I have to,
We have to.
I will,
we will.
I should,
we should.
Because I know I still have these traits,
I know you have these traits.
So let's share them.
Set them free.
Grow our bubble.
Till we share it through the whole world.
What a wonderful world that would be.

What Is It?

What is it?
What's on your mind?
You're in a foggy haze of some sort.
You're not stuck.
You want to stay there for a while.
Feels like you are not here.
And it's OK.
It's not scary.
You don't want interruption.
You want to go through it.
But why are you there?
What are you doing?
What do you want?
What do you see there?
Or better yet,
What's the best way to use this trance?
Why is it important to you?
How do you know you gained what you were looking for?
You can answer this:
You are grateful for this trance.
It feels like a direct path for possibilities.
Like your dreams already came true.
Like you are floating in joy.
You see it.
You feel it.
Everything is possible.
Everything is doable.
Everything is OK.
What else do you want?
What else can you achieve?

You can do it.
Just do it.
And be grateful for it.
Because you are guided.
You are protected.
You are OK.
Calm down.
Move forward.
Be OK with where you are now and keep going.
You will get there.
And you will smile.
You are smiling already.
Because you know what's coming.
You have your answer.
And suddenly,
Your pain, your sorrow, your despair,
It's all gone.
Now you feel safe, calm, happy, grateful, and you are sure that everything is possible.
So keep going.
Thank you for entering the trance.
Now keep going.
Move along your journey and believe that you reached your dream.
You did.
Not that you will.
But you already are.

Suffering in Silence Is All Kinds of Bad.

Suffering in silence is painful and draining and lonely.
Not many can share their suffering.
Some prefer to hide it and deal with it in dignity.
It's hard when you are in pain, and you can't show it.
When you are suffering, and you can't share it.
When you are lonely, and you have to be around people.
When you are lost, and you have to show confidence.
When you are in deep sorrow, and you have to put on a smile.
I get it.
The world wants a strong person.
Confident,
Tolerant,
Patient,
Forgiving,
A whole lot of bravery and openness.
Yet the moment they see your dark side,
They take a step back.
Some walk away.
Not many stick around.
Not many accept the real you.
Not many.
It's a hard realization.
That people don't accept you with all your virtues and all your flaws.
Yeah, some say they do.
But in reality, they don't.
So you choose to hide it.

Not for fear of rejection,
But for accepting and dealing with it alone on your own,
In silence.
I just wish for you to find your peace and your way,
On your own,
And move forward from there.
I also wish for you to find that one person,
Or crowd,
Who can stand by you when you need them.
Because that's what you would do for them.
Because you know that pain.
And you can help yourself,
And them.

Can't Sugarcoat It

There it is,
You can't hide it anymore.
That darkness creeping up inside.
You hid it so well.
Or so it seemed.
Then when it showed,
People were confused:
What's going on inside that head of yours?
You're not the sharing type.
Compose yourself.
Put on that smile.
Comment on something.
A joke really works.
They can't see the battle you carry inside you.
They wouldn't understand.
Your loved ones might think it's their fault.
Random people will say it's yours.
People who don't like you so much will say you got what you deserved.
But is it?
What you deserve?
Why?

You deserve better.
You know it's a phase.
Where you fall down,
And must find your way up.
For the sake of those who love you and care about you,
To show random people they don't know better.
To show people who don't really like you that you can come

back stronger than before.
Get up.
Stop giving up.
Stop feeling stuck.
Move.
Accept it and move.
Life is a tidal storm that calms down and rises up again.
You've been under the waves before.
Screaming in silence.
Fighting in stillness.
Drowning in despair.
Get up.
Look for the signs.
Look for the silver lining.
Look for it.
Find it.
Don't wait for it to find you.
You must.
Just have faith,
That the storm will pass,
As those before it always did.
And you came out of them a grateful winner.
Remember that.
Always.

Have Faith

A message from your future self:
Remember those days when you felt so dark,
And you never saw a way out.
Remember when you wondered if dying was the best answer to stop the pain.

Thankfully,
You had faith.
To know that everything happens for a reason.
You suffered greatly.
It was painful.
I know.
God knows how painful that was.
God knows how painful it all was.
Remember how many times you hit rock bottom,
And every time you'll say;
I never fell down that deep.
Yet somehow with faith,
Perseverance,
Hope,
And inner will,
You got up,
You fought back,
You pushed through,
And you won,
And you won big.
I know.
You wished you didn't have to struggle so much to win big.
But you know what,
Where you are now,

You know it was worth the fight.
Because seeing what you've become,
Made it worthwhile.
I know,
It hurts,
A lot.
But look how happy and grateful you are now.
You believed,
And now you shall receive.
You received the joy,
The solitude,
The love,
The appreciation,
The respect,
And all that you lost was doubled and tripled back to you.
So hang in there and have faith,
Be patient,
And keep believing.
You will get there.
You are already there.

P.S. I know it's gloomy and dark,
But it's about time to face reality and wake yourself up.

I Don't Know

It seems like you lost yourself somewhere along the way.
Not sure where.
Not sure when.
Not sure how.
Not sure what.

But somehow,
You don't recognize your life,
Yourself,
Your surroundings.
You don't hate the new you.
It's just that, you are feeling so different that its confusing you.
You've adapted so well to where you are,
That you didn't notice how much you have changed.
The question is:
Do you want to go back?
You know you don't.
But what are you looking for?
What are you missing?
Or at least,
What do you suddenly think is missing?
Figure it out.
It's draining you.
And it doesn't seem worth it.
Where you are right now is worth it.
And where you can be in the future Is worth even more.
Believe it.
See it.
Feel it.

Touch it.
God knows you will just pull yourself together.
People are depending on you.
You are depending on you.
Let go of the darkness.
It's OK.
Let go.
Let the light back in.
It will be too bright at the beginning,
But its warmth is beautiful.
You'll see.
You'll remember it.

P.S. I know you miss you.
I know you miss your family.
I know you miss being happy with your loved ones.

Hang in there.
It gets easier.

Well Then, We Wrote a New Story.

There now,
It's OK,
Cry it out.
Your relief,
Your joy,
Your sense of achievement,
Your sense of success.
You did it,
You changed your story,
You stopped your past from dictating your present and becoming your future.
Yes, there were bumps along the line.
Some big blocks,
But you pushed through,
You shifted the way you think.
You are so grateful and glad that you did.
Take it in,
Take a pause,
Breathe it in,
This moment,
This feeling,
Of freedom,
Of peace,
Of relaxation,
Of pausing to breathe,
Of being able to do that.
Alhamdulillah.
God was, is, and will be with us in every step.
Alhamdulillah for believing.
Alhamdulillah for achieving.

I can't even read at the moment.
It feels like a glimpse of the future,
Where I see myself succeeding.
Is it done?
I hope so.
I know it will end well.
It always does.

Stand Tall

Are you done?
Feeling bad?
Feeling sad?
Feeling scared?
Feeling lost?
Feeling confused?
Feeling consumed?

Now stand up.
Stand tall.

Pick up the pieces.
Wipe your tears.
You missed a spot.
Compose yourself.
Pull yourself together.
Now stand up.
Stand tall.
Face your fear.
Face the music.
Yes, the music.
You thought it was bangs and screams.
Yes, it's scary at first.
It just took you a bit longer to dance to the music.
I know it hurts.
But look at you.
You endured it.
It barely stings now.
I know it doesn't make it better,
But it makes it bearable.
And you found a way to get over the pain,

Over the noise,
Over the confusion,
And to move forward.
I tried to explain it to you.
But some things in life,
You can't learn unless you go through them.
So suck it up,
And get up,
And stand up,
And stand tall.

Don't We All

We stumble and fall,
Yet we stand up tall.
We don't think we need help,
But don't we all?
But do we ask for it?
Not at all.
Because of that, we stumble and fall.
But who do we call?
No one at all.
It's hard you know,
Knowing it all.
You keep trying and hoping not to fall,
But can you help it?
Not at all.
Please take the step,
Before you fall,
And make the call.
And slam your fear against the wall,
For there's enough love,
To cover us all,
And stop us somehow from that ugly fall.

Funny How Life Goes

It's funny,
How life knocks you down,
Stomps all over you.
Beats you down and cripples you with fear.
Makes you feel helpless and hopeless.
Until you decide that you can fight back,
That you can stand up to it.
Then suddenly,
You realize the world is just another big bully that was scaring you off to see how you can face your fear.
And all you have to do is face it and see it fade into dust.
And when it throws another curveball your way,
You realize you are much stronger to face it,
And you are more aware that it's an attempt to bring you back down again.
Fight it.
Keep fighting.
It's worth it.
It's easier than you think.
It's just your fear playing tricks on you.

Parenting Is Weird

It's funny,
How you swear as a child,
Not to repeat the mistakes your parents made in raising you.
Yet with time, you find yourself struggling not to follow in their footsteps.
Even worse, you find yourself doing all the things you swore you wouldn't do to your child.

What do you do then?
How do you stop, and do something else?
God. I swear it isn't easy. But you have got to try.
Most importantly, you need to notice that you are doing something wrong.
And find a way outside your comfort zone to fix it.

At least you noticed it.
Now change it.
It doesn't have to be drastic or different.
Just don't do it.
Sometimes not doing it is a change in and of itself.
Who am I kidding!
Writing it sounds so easy.
But behind these lines is a struggle that can last for days, weeks and months.
Just remind yourself:
Parenting is not an overnight habit that you suddenly start and are all OK with.
Parenting is a process.
Physical,
Mental,

Psychological,
Mechanical,
Functional.
You name it.
It takes everything you know and don't know to make it work.
And when it doesn't,
You find another way to make it work even better.

Alhamdulillah aala kul Hal (Thank God for Everything)

You know,
Life is scary.
It puts you down, then you fight and get back up again.
Then it puts you down then you get back again.
Until suddenly it stops being painful or scary or tiring.
It suddenly feels,
Normal.
Which shouldn't be.
But it is.
And you find yourself getting up,
Brushing off your shoulders
And moving along like it's a normal day.
Like nothing happened.
To the extent that you are so prepared,
When the second bump in the road comes.
It's unexpected,
In so many ways,
And it's bad in so many ways;
But you are so in control of yourself, so believing in God, and that everything happens for a reason;
You just find yourself laughing.
Yes, laughing.
No, you are not high,
No, you are not drunk.
You are just at peace.
Well, you were chuckling because it was so sudden and massive, and it was so OK,
You are laughing because it actually didn't scare you, but you didn't see it coming.

And when it did, it just felt like:
OK, that was not supposed to happen, but it did,
So it was meant to be this way, not your way.
So it's funny because it's confusing, when you add one and one you get 14…
Somehow deep inside.
You see your fear, your panic, but you just find your calm,
You find your core and you hear yourself say:
Everything happens for a reason.
You don't know it now,
But you will know it when it's right.
And deep down inside, you know that the puzzle pieces are falling apart.
Or in this case, the Lego pieces are falling apart;
Because you are about to build a new set of something,
Of everything.
Whether it's a home, a job, a life, a friendship.
Whatever it is you see is falling apart.
You have it in you already.
To believe that it's being broken down to be rebuilt into something new.
Something wonderful.
But you just don't see it yet.
When the time comes, you will know it.
Because you will see it.
It's scary.
Like your safety net is disappearing.
But seeing where you've been and where you are now,
Alhamdulillah, that things will get better and better sooner than you think.
Wait for it to unfold.
And enjoy the view.
You might learn something.

Watch It Grow

This is where the tides shift,
And you see it grow.
This is where your change starts,
And you never look back.
This is when you move forward, and you are as proud and as blessed as you can ever be.
الحمد لله رب العالمين

Keep Your Faith

Not sure what to do?
Not sure why things keep going the wrong way?
Then keep your faith.
Keep searching.
Keep fighting.
With all that happens, your energy might get depleted.
Charge your battery.
Keep your faith.

You will fall.
You will be tested.
And you will keep trying, over and over.
But listen to this first.
Ask yourself:
Am I worshiping God enough?
Am I fixing my mistakes?
Is there something I should be doing that I am not?
If your answers for these questions were, yes, yes, no,
Then try this:
Change something.
The thing is,
Without knowing, our prayers become habits,
Sometimes they become routine.
Not that it doesn't work.
It does, but you get so used to the same prayer that you do it out of habit, not belief.
So change it.
Search more.
Believe more.
Believe differently.

To simplify it:
If you are someone who is used to praying a lot, then add fasting.
If you are used to reading your prayers in the morning only,
Add an extra one midday.
If you are someone who likes to learn,
Search for a new lesson in your religion that you didn't know before.
We don't try with God.
We believe it works when the time is right.
But we can worship our God better.

You will go through a lot in life.
You will need a lot of tools in your hands.
The reason faith and religion are the tools to focus on
Is because some days you lose big losses
But with faith in your heart,
You will find ways to build your own tools,
And move forward,
And keep fighting.
Hopefully you will not lose that much,
But if you do and if you don't,
Keep faith in your heart.
Forever and always.

Listen to Your Heart, Faithfully

There's so much happening.
Things that were wrong are OK.
Things that were OK are wrong.
It's reaching a point where we are questioning our own basic principles.
And that's a big problem.
When what you believe seems to be wrong or untrue,
Where do you go from there?
Am I with it?
Or against it?
I can't decide.
And that's what scares me the most.
But here's what I will do,
And here's what I urge you to do.
Search.
Research.
Read.
Reread.
Investigate.
Ask.
Question.
Go back to the roots,
See where things went wrong.
Make sure they are solid.
That you are solid.
And you know for sure,
What's right and what's wrong.

If something is new,
Learn it.

Study it well.
Go back to your roots.
Compare and contrast.
Until you are sure that this new knowledge goes with your roots—
Not against it.

And most of all:
Don't follow blindly.
Because not everyone who seems like they know, actually know everything.
Follow your heart,
And listen to it faithfully.
Find the right path and follow it.
And ask for guidance,
Because these days it's easy to get lost.
I pray you always find your way back to the right path.

Have Meaning

We all look for deep meaning and value in our lives.
Living for the moment will stop being fulfilling at some point.
You will ask yourself,
What's next?
Why am I here?
Is this what I want?
Is this all I want?
Isn't there more?
Not in terms of greed,
But in terms of value?

If You Weren't Afraid

What would you do if you weren't afraid?
Do you think that you aren't afraid?
Oh, but you are.
You just don't know it.
You think your wounds have healed,
But when faced with them,
You realize how scared you still are.
Your trauma was big.
You survived.
You lived on.
You stood tall.
But a part of you still feels haunted,
Crippled,
Paralyzed,
Frozen in that moment of fear.
You need to move from there.
You need to get unstuck.
How do you get unstuck?
You got bigger.
You got better.
Then why are you still frozen by that moment?
Maybe you are afraid to feel that pain again?
But look around,
You had other pains,
That you pulled through,
Some were even worse.
Or,
Wait a minute,
Are you still stuck in all of them,
And are just pretending that you moved on?

Why are you stuck there?
Let it be.
It happened then and there.
You are here now.
Or,
Is it,
That you are afraid to feel a similar pain?
A similar shock?
A similar disappointment?
True,
You never know what will come next.
You know some pains were huge,
And you came out of them,
Strongly.
Beautifully.
Bravely.
Faithfully.
You are not afraid of that moment,
You are afraid of the pain that might happen if you relive a similar moment.
Don't.
You are the one losing.
It's ok.
Go ahead,
And try again,
Try to live,
It will be ok.
You are doing great.
If the pain comes again,
You will be ok with it,
And you will pull through.
And if it doesn't,

Well,
Look at what you gained,
And how wonderful it can be.
Count your blessings after that moment,
You will find there are plenty to go around.
Set yourself free of that moment.
You deserve it.
You owe it to yourself to do so.

A Matter of Perspective

Sometimes, the way we live life,
It's nothing more than our mere perspective of things.
One way to look at things,
Is to push for what you think and believe is right.
On the other side,
You might just be stubborn and missing out on a few key points,
That leave you misguided,
With a wrong purpose…

Love Is Your Sticky Tape

Life throws us some challenging curveballs.
They test our togetherness to the core.
With love as your sticky tape,
You tend to patch your relationship and commitment to one another to keep going.
"Love isn't enough" comes as a realization;
That with all that happens between a man and a woman,
You need to use your love as your Band-Aid and your goodness as your ointment to keep that relationship going.
Love isn't enough,
But it's your sticky tape that keeps you glued to each other,
And to your kids, and to who you wanted to be, And who you still want to continue being for one another.
People nowadays seem to fear the commitment of marriage, kids and responsibility.
It became easier to commit to oneself or to half a relationship, and not to the full package.
Try to see the goodness in the big picture;
Look at grandparents, and how happy they look seeing their kids and their grandkids.
It shows you a different kind of purpose and self-achievement that you can only see through the eyes of the people you love, and who love you back.
Take a step forward and commit to your family.
Have the belief that they are worth your time and effort.
And commit to yourself along the way.
Because self-love is a part of family love.
It goes a long way.

A House of Keys 1

Imagine living in a house of keys.
Keys for everything you dream of.
Keys for fun.
Keys for joy.
Keys for stunts.
Keys for positivity.
Keys for today.
Keys for tomorrow.
Imagine living in a house of keys,
Where every key takes you to a room of wonder,
A room of hope,
A room of love,
A room of faith,
A room of peace,
A room of possibilities.
A room of options,
where everything is possible and everything is positive.
I wonder what else would be there?
Would there be a key for sadness?
And another for pain?
Would there be a key for anger?
And another for self-gain?
Maybe all keys should open all types of possibilities.
Maybe through the key of sorrow we will find the key of joy.
Through fear we'll find safety.
Through hate we'll find love.
What keys will you find in the house of keys?
Or maybe,
What keys will you *want* to have found in the house of keys?

The House of Keys 2

What if you lived in a house of keys?
Where there is a key for everything you need?
What if you lived in a house of keys?
Where all possibilities can be seen?
What happens now?
What happens then?
With all your dreams and all your needs,
It all comes down to a turn of keys.
What would you choose, what would you do?
I wish I could share my house of keys.
But it's mine and mine to keep.
Because I know that you will find yours.
And you will have more to be grateful for.
Just keep trying and keep searching.
For the house of keys will be worth your while.

What Was the Question Again?

I am my question and my question is me.
I know it's confusing but so are we.
There are moments when I wonder and try to see.
What questions would matter and would mean to me.
Sometimes it's so deep that we can't even see,
What answers are there, and what might it be?
So give yourself a chance to ask and to see,
And what answer might come, just let it be.
For these questions will determine and become what we see,
They also give us a change of heart and set our spirits free.
So it's ok to ask the question and change what you may be.
For the question is me,
And what I may just be.

Happy or Sad

Mother: Honey, you need to learn to do this on your own.
As if I am not here.
Kid: you are always here Mommy.
Mother: what if I am not. What would you do? You need to know how to do this alone.
Kid: you are always here Mommy I know you are.
Mother: what if I am not. I am not with you in school.
Kid: you always show up Mommy.
Mother: …(confused) well let's pretend that I don't…. As if….
Kid: you show up Mommy.
Mother: let's just focus on what needs to be done.
From this moment forward, the mother is as confused as she could be.
Should she be proud to have provided the level of safety and trust her kids gave her—
That she is always there when they need her?
Or did she just cripple them to always need her to save them or solve their problems?
Should she find ways to disappoint them and break that trust,
So they can depend on themselves and be strong to face anything that comes along their way?
Well, they should be independent.
But how can it be done without the burden of feeling guilty, like their safety net is not there?
Or is it just the wrong way of thinking…
Wondering how to fix that?
Still working on it.

How can we teach our kids to listen?

You can't wish for your kids that something bad happens so they learn about the danger around them.
You can only warn them, and give them the space to stumble and fall if the fall isn't that dangerously steep.
They can touch a warm cup to know it can be hot, Instead of touching a boiling pot to know that it's hot.
You can pretend not to notice them holding the scissors, and watch silently as they cut a magazine (not their homework) so they understand that the scissors are for cutting *some* papers, not all.
Well, the examples are endless, so find a way to let go of their hands gently,
Until the day they let go on their own;
Without having to feel the anxiety of letting go, or wondering how they will succeed.
It takes practice, trial and error, stumbles and mistakes, till both sides get it right, mother and child.

Freeze

Sometimes,
You just want the world to take a pause;
To freeze,
To stop,
Rotating;
But it doesn't.
You need,
A moment;
To fathom,
What's going on;
What just happened?
To ask yourself,
Where are you?
What are you doing?
To figure out,
What will you do?
What happens next?
But it doesn't.
It keeps revolving.
You have your meetings, family, and social events.
You actually have to wake up and shower and put a smile on your face.
It's not depression.
You are exactly where you want to be.
You just need to know what happens next,
Or who you become from that moment forward.
But the world keeps moving;
Don't you wish for the world to stand still?
Just for a minute;
But it doesn't.

And you can't,
You keep moving along with it,
No matter what.
What happens next?
Well,
Maybe the world keeps moving so you don't get stuck.
So you don't freeze in the moment.
And you just ask yourself,
Where can you go from here?
Where do you want to go from here—
Isn't that a better question to consider?
You've planned so much to reach this moment, Where you
did everything right before some things went wrong,
And you got it.
So,
Why stop now?
Plan again,
Plan ahead.
Go on forward.
Maybe not everything on your bucket list is completed,
But look at it, almost all done.
So make a new one.
A more lasting one,
A continuous cycle;
And see where you can move on from there.

A Lesson in Life

Try something.
If it doesn't work,
Then there is a mistake there somewhere,
Find it,
Fix it,
Then try again,
Until you get it right.
It's not giving up,
It's not stubbornness,
Its agility, stamina, grit, and the will to keep going till you get it right and go to the next phase.

The Day I Failed in Everything

One day, everything crumbled
Marriage
Parenting
Fashion business
Coaching
Home management
Just suddenly, everything fell apart.
All of that over, 5000 SR…
Yup.
So trivial, but it happened.
Such a hard day that was.
Grateful to God that it was a simple mistake that passed.
Just the drama associated with it was so big, that I realized how fragile I was.
I didn't think that I was drowning in responsibilities and fixing things as they come along and get damaged,
But I realized that day that I was fixing outwards more than I was fixing inwards
Everything was in place really, home, husband, kids, work,
But it seemed like the pressure of keeping everything afloat just reached its limit that day.
It passed really,
But it showed me that I need to take care of me internally,
As much as I am taking care of everything and everyone externally.
Not sure yet how to do that, still working on it,
But now it's on my radar just like the rest of my tasks, not hidden on the upper shelf or in the side drawer.

Can You Let People Learn Their Own Lessons?

We all have our own journeys that teach us how to move forward through situations.
You keep reminding yourself that we all have our own cycles to go through;
Our own lessons to learn in life.
Some start their lessons early.
Some have a certain progression that seems like a textbook progression.
Others have it happen as they go along. No basic steps to follow.
You reached a few realizations recently about life lessons;
Some of us learn it early on in life,
Some of us learn it a bit late.
Some of us get the lesson, and do better the second time around.
Some of us don't get the lesson, and keep stumbling at the same obstacle until we actually give up.

This is where your confusion comes.
Having gone through some lessons earlier than you hoped you would,
Sometimes you see some people stuck and you just want to pull them out of there and tell them:
Read the signs!
See the labels!

Follow the instructions!

Then, recently (with the help of coaching, religion, self-exploration, and loads and loads of research) You got to the realization
That you can't help them,
Like they couldn't help you when you first got the warning, and still stumbled and fell.
I guess you had to fall to understand the message.
Some messages, you understood the warnings and avoided the bumps in the road;
Others, you stumbled and fell.
It's all part of your learning journey to do better.
It's not easy seeing people around you, being misguided, thinking they know better, when you know they don't.
But somehow, you wonder, who am I to show them better, when it's their journey, and their enlightenment.
Sometimes, it really isn't your place to show them.
Maybe showing them will ruin a lesson that can end beautifully.
But then again.
Some people just don't get it.
These situations make you want to grab the next person and scream at them to wake up and read the signs.
But it isn't your place, not out of weakness, or giving up,
But from having a deeper understanding and appreciation for our own individual journeys.
That being said—how can you as a parent, as a sibling, as someone's daughter or son or cousin or friend, see them drown and just stand by and watch.
Where and when is that choice, to step in and or stand by; still baffles you, really.

But I guess that where and when you interfere, and it works, is where and when it was meant to be for it to work. And when it doesn't, then you pray to God that they find their answer and move forward with their lives.

A Blast from the Near Past 1: What's Next? After 96 Days?

96 days of lockdown;
I don't know what's next.
Tomorrow is the first day since the corona drama started and the country decided to lift the quarantine.
Numbers are still high.
It decreased a bit.
There is news of a medicine that is helpful.
There is news of a vaccine in progress.
There was news before of a malaria medicine being used.
There's a new medicine that they said is working, which is actually a cortisone medicine that's already available.
They say it will be produced for the masses, in large quantities.
People are excited that quarantine is over.
But I think it's scary.
What if people are reckless?
The disease isn't over yet…
I hope people are smart.
I hope people think of their loved ones first.
I hope things turn out better than we hope.

A Blast from the Near Past 2: So What Will It Be?

If you hear the phrase:
"Corona Drama", know that this is my statement for all that's happening around.
I still don't know if it is a blessing or a curse.
A lot of people suffered.
A lot of realities were revealed.
A lot of people were enlightened.
One way or another.
Everyone was affected by the corona drama.
The question now is:
Which part of the story do you belong to so far?
Did you get sick?
How bad was it?
Which symptoms did you get?
Did you quarantine yourself?
Were you immune?
Did you lose your job?
Were you hired?
Did you save your home?
Were you evicted or kicked out or separated or divorced?
Did you learn anything?
Were you laid back?
Did you freak out?
Were you careful?
Did you believe all the news?
Were you convinced by the conspiracy theory?
Did you survive?
Were you damaged?

Did you lose a loved one?
We will go down in history,
As a generation who faced a plague or pandemic or whatever they call it,
And still some people think it's fake...
So which story will you tell?
What's your story?

We are lucky to still be around,
We are lucky to still be afloat.
We are lucky to have survived and found a way to move forward.
People suffered.
People died.
You survived for a reason.
Keep moving forward and make a positive change in the world.

A Blast from the Near Past 3: A Lot of "I Don't Know"

To be honest,
A lot has been going on.
On a personal level,
Economic level,
Pandemic level,
Family level.
The one thing I can say about all of this, is this:
I don't know.
I don't know what to expect.
I don't know what's next.
I don't know what to do.
I don't know what's right.
I don't know what I am doing wrong.
I don't know where my mistake is.
I don't know how to make it better.
I don't know how to think outside the box and change my perspective.
I don't know if I can handle the pressure much longer.
I don't know anything.
I don't know everything.
I missed my pages,
Where what I see is what I put there.
No surprises.
No sudden change in events.
My pages offer the subtle truth I look for.
I don't know what my truth is now.
I came to terms with it.
I accept it.

I want to say it's OK.
But it isn't.
I am struggling as a parent, as a wife, as an entrepreneur, as a coach, as a person in general.
It's too much to think about and work through,
Especially when there are no breaks in between.
But,
I really love positivity in life.
So,
the positive notes are:
I am surviving.
I am grateful I can put my business on hold,
And my coaching practice and my book too,
So I can give my attention to my family.
All of that is without losing more,
I learned (still learning) a certain level of acceptance,
That I can't do everything at once.
I learned that for some reason,
Along the way,
I learned that if one way isn't working,
Try another way;
Not the same way over and over again.
What's next?
I don't know.
I am taking it one day or week at a time.
I can't even plan for a month with everything happening around me.
But I will get there.
I will succeed like I always do.
Because I believe.
You should believe too.

Ending This with a Wish

If I am leaving myself with a message to remember from this book:
Always question.
Always believe in what's good.
Always keep trying.
Listen to criticism—you will learn something that makes you better.
Look for a higher purpose, getting rich isn't one.
Leave a mark for people to remember you by,
To follow in your footsteps with, and to thank you for it for years to come.
If certain situations are a bit hard,
Look closely,
Maybe you didn't notice the lesson yet.
Keep going,
With a purpose,
You will get there,
And when you do get there,
Keep going forward for a new goal, for a higher purpose.
You are here for a reason,
Figure it out,
And use it for the good of mankind.
We all have a message to figure out and deliver.
But we have to find it out on our own by reading the signs.
We have to read on our own.
After all, going up is interpreted differently by each and every one of us.
That's the beauty of life.

Read the Message

No matter how deep you are,
In trouble,
In pain,
In sorrow,
In disgust,
In anger,
In denial.
Just try,
Go back to the question:
What's going on here?
Ask the question of:
Why is this happening?
Not out of ungratefulness or despair,
But out of concern,
To try to understand the message it carries.
If it still seems hard to ask that question, try this one:
What can I learn from this?
How can I grow from here?
What can I take as lessons learned?
Believe me,
Once you answer that question,
And you know within your heart that this happened in order for you to grow,
Use that chance and grow bigger.
And you will notice that things will get easier.
Things will progress smoothly,
And somehow, you won't take as much time being stuck as you used to.
I am grateful,
That I have reached this enlightenment.

Keep going,
Keep growing.
For as random as life can be,
As random as your trip can help you grow…

We hope you enjoyed the read!

Find new such reads and reads
in many other genres in our store:
https://sailpublishing.com/store/

Follow us on our social media
to stay updated with our news:
Instagram: @SailPublishing
Twitter: @SailPublishing
Facebook: facebook.com/SailPublishing

For any queries, email us on:
info@SailPublishing.com

www.ingramcontent.com/pod-product-compliance
Lightning Source LLC
LaVergne TN
LVHW090535110826
845146LV00003B/1109

* 9 7 9 8 9 8 9 3 7 7 5 2 7 *